FREYA STEPHENS

how to grow your
emotional
intelligence

PRACTICAL TIPS AND GUIDED
EXERCISES TO BOOST YOUR EQ

HOW TO GROW YOUR EMOTIONAL INTELLIGENCE

Copyright © Octopus Publishing Group Limited, 2024

Text by Caroline Roope

An Hachette UK Company
www.hachette.co.uk

Vie Books, an imprint of Summersdale Publishers
Part of Octopus Publishing Group Limited
Carmelite House
50 Victoria Embankment
LONDON
EC4Y 0DZ
UK

www.summersdale.com

This FSC® label means
that materials used for
the product have been
responsibly sourced

MIX
Paper | Supporting
responsible forestry
FSC® C018236

The authorized representative in the EEA is Hachette Ireland, 8 Castlecourt Centre, Castleknock Road, Castleknock, Dublin 15, D15 YF6A, Ireland

Printed and bound in Poland

ISBN: 978-1-83799-396-3

Substantial discounts on bulk quantities of Summersdale books are available to corporations, professional associations and other organizations. For details contact general enquiries: telephone: +44 (0) 1243 771107 or email: enquiries@summersdale.com.

Contents

Introduction

Emotional intelligence (or EQ) is the ability to perceive, use, understand and manage emotions. It's about using your emotions intelligently and deploying that knowledge to better manage your thoughts and behaviours, as well as improving your ability to communicate with others.

The skills you need for a higher EQ are increasingly valued in the modern world – especially in workplaces, where building positive, productive connections with others is fundamental to success. Research suggests that employees with lower levels of emotional intelligence are more likely to report worse well-being, commitment levels, job satisfaction and performance at work, along with more job-related stress.

Unlike cognitive intelligence – a measure of our mental abilities – emotional intelligence refers to how we respond emotionally to situations and other people. In a workplace study, over 70 per cent of employers commented that they value EQ over IQ, and 75 per cent were more likely to promote an employee with a high EQ over a worker with a high IQ. So, with stats like this, it's a part of ourselves that we can't afford to ignore. Outside of the workplace, it's also been proven that EQ helps us to build stronger, more authentic relationships, boost our confidence and levels of resilience, and develop better communication and negotiation skills.

The great news is that anyone can improve their emotional intelligence – you just need a bit of self-awareness, a little effort and a steer in the right direction. Psychologists divide the skill sets needed for a high EQ into four key areas: self-awareness, self-regulation, social awareness and relationship management – and you'll find a section on each of these in this book.

Using a combination of tips, simple activities and inspirational words, you'll learn how to harness your emotions so that they have a positive impact on your life, as well as helping you to develop the skills you need to understand and react to the emotions of others.

Sound good? Let's begin...

Chapter 1:

How to Develop Self-Awareness

Self-awareness is our ability to understand and be aware of our unique self: our emotions, actions and experiences – and the effect these have on other people. You could say that they form the foundation stone of emotional intelligence from which we can build and develop our self-regulation, social awareness and relationship management. When we truly know ourselves, we are more confident and make sounder decisions. We're also better communicators, which helps us build stronger relationships with others. Make self-awareness your superpower, with some help from the following pages.

Understanding
emotions is a journey.
Possibly an adventure.
When it's finished,
we may find ourselves
someplace new.

MARC BRACKETT

Hello, you!

How well do you know yourself? It sounds like an odd question, but a study conducted by organizational psychologist Tasha Eurich found that although 95 per cent of those who took part believed they were self-aware, in fact only 10–15 per cent actually were – making it a surprisingly rare quality! Which begs the question: considering we spend all our time in our own company, why are we so bad at knowing ourselves?

Here are some of the reasons:

- We're not the best judge of our own characters and find it difficult to admit to our flaws.

- We live in fear of being judged or perceived in a certain way, which can lead us to conceal our faults, consciously or unconsciously.

- We're not particularly good at remembering things correctly. This can be because of unconscious bias (see the next point) or simply because each time we relive a memory, it can be a slightly different version of the event. Tiny mistakes or embellishments might creep in, influenced by what we believe or wish was true and other people's recollections. And whenever this happens, it can affect the recall of that memory later.

- We're often a product of society and carry around deep-rooted biases based on our upbringing, life experiences, values, beliefs and relationships with others. This means we actively look for information that supports a pre-existing conviction and tend to disregard anything that doesn't – our views and opinions can become unbalanced.

- We still behave like cavemen if we're put in a challenging situation – we feel scared, like our ancestors, when confronted with a threat, even though we might just be going to a job interview. In other words, our life-saving functions get in the way of our ability to be self-aware enough to manage our emotions and the situation.

But the good news is that self-awareness can be learned if we're willing to put our inner selves under a microscope. Exploring our thoughts like this can evoke conflicting emotions, but being receptive to what we're feeling – good and bad – can provide an amazing insight into who we really are. And it's only through discovering our authentic selves that we can begin to enhance our lives with emotional intelligence.

Q and A

Asking ourselves some simple questions and answering them truthfully can help us uncover our own inner world, which means we're a step closer to understanding what makes us, well... us.

Answer the following questions with the first response that pops into your head. The capacity to keep an open mind about your responses – whether they make sense right now or not – is self-awareness in action and your first step towards greater emotional intelligence.

I am a person who...

Is inspired by...	Is afraid of...
Wants to...	Loves to...
Hates to...	Believes in...
Is happiest when...	Gets upset when...

I want, by understanding
myself, to understand others.

Katherine Mansfield

Suss out your strengths, work out your weaknesses

Identifying your strengths and weaknesses can be a really valuable exercise for self-awareness. Not only will it help you become better acquainted with the qualities that make you *you*, but it'll also allow you to approach tasks and challenges with a better understanding of how to succeed and the personal pitfalls you might need to look out for. It also provides a helpful insight into what you can contribute to everyday situations – at college, work and even at home – and how best to communicate that to those around you.

How to do it:

- Set aside 20–30 minutes of undisturbed time when you are fully focused on the task and your mind is clear enough to really probe. On the next page, you'll find some space to record your thoughts.

- Think of two separate experiences in your life – one that went really well (such as an event you organized that went to plan or nailing a job interview) and one that went badly (for example, a teamwork exercise that fell apart or a poorly organized day trip with friends).

- Next, ask yourself what strengths and skills you demonstrated that enabled you to succeed and what weaknesses may have contributed to your unsuccessful experience. What else could you have contributed to both situations? What could you have done differently? If it was a shared experience, what did other people think of your contribution?

If you're not sure you can be truly objective about yourself, you could try asking a trusted but honest friend or relative to provide feedback on your strengths and weaknesses. It can be tough to listen to criticism, but if it's constructive and helpful, it'll give you further insight into how others perceive you. Often, an outside perspective can be illuminating, but don't forget it is just their opinion and doesn't necessarily mean they are right. Reflect on whether you agree with them or not – and if you don't, it might be helpful to consider why they might think that way.

Strengths

_____

_____

_____

_____

_____

Weaknessess

_____

_____

_____

_____

_____

Accepting the gift of feedback

Listening to feedback or a critique of something you've done can be tough. But if we're open to receiving feedback, it can be a window into understanding how our behaviours and actions impact on the people around us – which is vital for increasing self-awareness. Not only that, it's also a good way to grow as a person – more effective than any insight we could get from reading books, academic journal articles, training and speeches, according to organizational psychologist David Burkus.

Constructive feedback can help you to:

- Become better at what you want to achieve.

- Make changes that can have a positive impact on your life.

- Earn the trust and respect of those around you.

- Improve personal and working relationships and become more effective at understanding the needs of others.

The four steps for accepting feedback

1 Say thank you. Don't get defensive or immediately try to explain. Offering thanks tells the other person that you're willing to listen.

2 Take the time to restate to the person giving the feedback what you heard them say so you can check your understanding of what they are telling you.

3 Consider what they said and reflect on how you can behave or act differently in the future.

4 Come up with your own personal plan for what changes you can make. Listening to feedback alone doesn't bring about growth; it's only by making changes and adjustments to ourselves that we grow as people.

Seek out more feedback opportunities. It isn't just a one-off gift! It's a process. You're growing and improving all the time – to do that, you'll need regular feedback.

At different stages of our lives, we'll be either giving or receiving feedback – or even both. Receiving feedback can be challenging for many of us, but doing so regularly, whether at college, work or from friends and family, really is the key to unlocking our full potential. That's why it's a gift!

Awareness is the greatest agent for change.

Eckhart Tolle

It's not your job to like
me – it's mine.

Byron Katie

Try a thought diary

Writing down your thoughts is an excellent way to increase self-awareness. Whether it's thinking about how irritating the noise of the neighbour's music is, or something more profound, such as whether civilization would be better off without the internet(!), getting your thoughts down onto paper can help you track what triggers them – as well as record any emotions you feel as a result. By writing down the thoughts and associated feelings, you can see any common threads emerging. You can then use that insight to help you manage your future response.

For example, perhaps Daisy is thinking about storming round the neighbour's house to complain about their music. She writes:

- **Thought:** *How much longer am I going to have to listen to this?*

- **I feel:** *Tense. Extremely irritable and angry. Like I want to move house right now!*

- **What I'm doing:** *Trying to write a college essay that is due in first thing tomorrow.*

In this case, it's not actually the noisy neighbour that is the issue, it's Daisy's own lack of organization and time management that has sent her into a spin. The neighbour's plan to listen to music is just an unhappy (if annoying) coincidence that has compounded her feelings of irritation.

TOP TIP

People naturally reflect on their thoughts and feelings with a self-serving bias rather than objectively. To make the most of your thought diary, it should be less of an emotional exercise and more of a fact-finding mission – so try to leave judgement out of it.

Self-awareness is
the first step towards
achieving your goals

When you are self-aware,
you are guided by your
thoughts
and
emotions

Mindful me

Mindfulness isn't just a way to relax and calm your mind – it's also a brilliant way to increase self-awareness. Just as self-awareness requires us to direct our thoughts inward, mindfulness can help us become aware of how we're feeling inside, which allows us to get comfortable acknowledging our emotions in our everyday lives. Studies show that mindfulness can help us nurture a positive self-attitude, leading to acceptance and self-compassion, which, in turn, help us to be equally compassionate to others. It can also help us tune into our emotional triggers and provides a safe mental space, when this happens, for us to explore and interpret what we're feeling – whether it's positive or negative.

When you practise mindfulness, your behaviour becomes more intentional, and – voilà – you've increased your self-awareness.

How to do it:

- Choose a peaceful location where you can sit or lie down, whichever is most comfortable.

- Close your eyes to avoid external distractions. Take some deep, calming breaths to restore your inner balance.

- Focus on the rhythm of your breathing. Acknowledge each inhale and exhale, and as you breathe, observe the sensation of your chest rising and falling.

- Notice your emotions and how you are feeling in the present moment, without judgement. Acknowledge the feeling by naming it in your head, but don't have an opinion on it – just let it float by.

- If your mind starts to wander, simply refocus on your breathing to bring yourself back to the present moment.

TOP TIP

Mindfulness works best when it's a regular habit. Once you've mastered the basics, try tagging it on to an existing healthy habit, such as after a yoga session or before you write your daily journal entry, to really make it stick.

What do you value?

Our values are the things that are important to us, such as honesty, optimism, compassion or resilience. They help guide our actions and decisions, which means they're fundamental to emotional intelligence and specific to each of us. When we reflect on our values, we're practising self-awareness. And once we know them, we can determine whether we're spending our time effectively and making decisions in accordance with what we find important.

One of the easiest ways to identify values is to ask yourself some questions:

- What is important to you?

- What would a perfect day look like? What values does this choice represent?

- What would you like to spend your free time doing?

- What do you enjoy doing?

- What would you do if there were no limitations?

The decisions your values inform could be fairly minor (choosing what to do with your free time) to something major (questioning whether to work for a company or not, based on an aligned ethos). There are no limits on how many values you have, but it can be useful to identify three core ones that can provide you with a starting point when faced with a dilemma. The context will always be significant, but having core values to lean on can help to signpost you towards a decision.

What is necessary
to change a person is to
change his awareness
of himself.

Abraham Maslow

You-logy

It might sound a little strange, but writing an imaginary eulogy for yourself can be illuminating. Recording how you'd like to be remembered after you're gone can be a really beneficial exercise for developing self-awareness. It allows you to consider what changes need to occur in your life if you're to live the existence you've eulogized, as well as providing an opportunity to look back and consider what you can learn from your experiences.

It will also help you to see the arc of your life journey from a different angle, and while you won't get to hear what people will say about you when you're gone, or control what they are planning to say, you can consider now, while you're still alive, what you would want to hear. And then make it your mission to live that life to the best of your ability.

Greater awareness
of how others perceive
you helps you to grow

Self-discovery journalling

Journalling is a little like a brain dump. Our minds are often so full of thoughts that it's difficult to see a clear path through all the clutter. Journalling allows us to gain the clarity and insight we need for personal growth. It's also been proven to reduce anxiety, promote feelings of wellness and help us to work out solutions when facing a challenge. Most importantly, if we use writing prompts that help us to discover our true selves, we'll be enhancing our self-awareness.

It's super simple to get started. All you need is some paper and a pen. As with any new habit, you'll need to commit to a few minutes a day to begin with, and you can always increase your writing time if you find it beneficial.

- Find a quiet and peaceful place to write.

- Write openly and freely – no one else will see it, so don't hold back!

- If you find typing easier, there are plenty of online journalling pages or apps you can use.

- Just let the words flow and write down anything that comes to mind.

- Use journal prompts if you need to – there are some on the following page.

- Be creative – use coloured pens, draw a picture, write a poem, or anything else that helps you express your thoughts.

- Take time to reflect on what you've written so that you can gain insight into your thoughts.

Pick a prompt

If you're not sure what to write first, choose one of these prompts to help get you started.

- Is there anything you regret not doing in life – and if so, why?

- What would your absolute best day look like and why?

- Describe how you are/were feeling today/yesterday.

- Name something you fear and why.

- Are you happy with your life? If not, is there something you should or want to change?

- How would you describe yourself from the perspective of a friend or loved one?

To remember who you are, you need to forget who you were told to be

OPPORTUNITIES ARE
A GIFT – EMBRACE ALL
THAT COME YOUR WAY

Reader, know your worth!

Self-esteem relates to how we value and perceive ourselves, and it is fundamental to our self-awareness. It's thought that up to 85 per cent of the world's population is affected by low self-esteem. That's an awful lot of people undervaluing themselves.

Our self-esteem exists on a scale. Where we are on that scale is influenced by the opinions and beliefs we hold about ourselves, which can have a negative or positive tone, depending on how healthy our self-esteem is. High self-esteem does not mean thinking you are the best at everything – rather, it's being comfortable with who you are, even when life isn't going to plan. It means having total self-acceptance of your strengths and weaknesses, as well as confidence in your own abilities. But more than anything else, it's about trusting and having faith in yourself.

We can raise our self-esteem by learning to like ourselves, which sounds simple, but the reality can be really tricky! Try these strategies to help improve your relationship with yourself and get your self-esteem up to a healthy level:

- Practise verbally asserting yourself – with friends, family members or co-workers – in ways that don't feel too intimidating. Perhaps you have always wanted to tell your colleague that you actually like your tea weaker than they usually make it. Maybe you need to turn down an offer for coffee with that friend who always assumes that, because you work from home, you have lots of free time. Remember, being assertive isn't the same as being arrogant – it's about making sure others recognize your needs, as well as expressing those needs clearly and calmly.

- Try to do something new or challenging, either daily or weekly.

- Give yourself a daily shot of self-praise – a simple "go you" works wonders.

- Be honest about your goals so you reduce the risk of disappointing yourself.

- Practise confident posture – make sure you're making good eye contact, smiling and standing straight. Get a trusted friend to give you a mini appraisal so you can get a sense of how others see you.

- Practise positive affirmations – you will find plenty of examples in this book for inspiration.

- Don't compare yourself to others; focus on self-improvement, not on always being "the best". Self-confidence comes from within, not from external validation.

Seek out positivity and use it to drive yourself

towards your goals

Fear nothing.
Do what you
want to do, but
be educated
and intelligent
and confident
about it.

Idris Elba

Bin your bad habits

We don't tend to give habits much thought. They're just something we do, often without question (especially if they're bad ones), but therein lies the problem! Here's the science: when you repeatedly do the same thing, it can feel comforting. The feel-good hormone dopamine is released in your body, and you get a little boost of pleasure. But while some habits might feel good, they may not actually be good for you. Being aware of those and taking steps to change your behaviour can help to increase your self-awareness.

If you know you've got some bad habits, you'll need to look out for:

- Their triggers – stress, anxiety, feeling low, being around certain people and the time of day are common factors that might make you want to reach for your personal habit-crutch. For example, spending too much time on social media.

- The things that make you engage in the habits you're trying to break. For example, you could stop scrolling and fill that time with a healthier habit.

- Opportunities to be more mindful of your thoughts and actions. For example, do you really need to reach for your phone?

Every day is a chance
to learn, grow and
stay open-minded

Self-awareness and relationships

Self-awareness is a crucial part of a healthy relationship. When we are self-aware, we're able to see ourselves clearly and objectively, which means we can be the best version of ourselves with those around us. Self-awareness boosts our decision-making and communication skills, as well as our self-confidence. It improves our compassion, allowing us to see other people's perspectives, too. It's also true that if we're happier within ourselves, we're more likely to form positive relationships with others. Conversely, self-awareness allows us to recognize when our flaws and weaknesses might be having a negative influence on those around us as well.

No one has a perfect consciousness of self. We're human – and not only does "perfect" not really exist, but we also have blind spots when it comes to ourselves. However, aiming to develop good self-awareness can benefit us and our relationships.

If you want to improve your self-awareness and nurture positive relationships, try these tips:

- **Don't overestimate yourself**. We often criticize others for lacking self-awareness but don't recognize it in ourselves. By reflecting on your feelings and behaviour in different situations, you can become aware of how you may have contributed to an issue.

- **Encourage communication**. The healthiest relationships involve balanced communication. No one likes to be critical of a loved one, and it's important you both feel comfortable discussing when one person's behaviour has had a negative impact on the other. Encourage open, honest and respectful communication.

- **Ask yourself questions.** When there is tension in a relationship, be it at work, at home or with friends, evaluate yourself by asking some probing questions, such as: "What else was happening that day for me to respond in that way?", "Was there a trigger?" and "What impact has that had on the other person?"

- **Discuss self-awareness**. Talking about what it is you want to improve in yourself and your relationship can help it to become a reality. Share this with your partner, a family member or a trusted friend, letting them know that you want to try to become more self-aware, and seek their support and feedback.

When we're self-aware, we're more tuned into the thoughts and feelings of others. This higher level of compassion allows us to be open, loving and supportive of our friends and loved ones.

Don't be afraid to take risks
and put yourself out there.
You have to be
an active participant.

Halima Aden

All you have to do is ask...

Understanding other people's perceptions of us is key to emotional intelligence. One of the best ways to get a balanced perspective is to ask fellow students or colleagues, family members and friends. Choose one trusted person from each group, and then, based on what they say, you can reflect on whether you need to modify any of your behaviours.

Remember that everyone's opinions are subjective, and EQ can help you recognize whether their feedback is useful or not. You can be comfortable with who you are *and* open to hearing other perspectives.

To start the conversation, be sincere and honest. You might say, "I'm working on my self-awareness, and I trust you to be objective." If they need a prompt, try asking some of the questions below:

- What three words best describe me?

- What's the best advice you've ever received from me?

- What's the number one thing you wish more people knew about me?

- What is something I do that you wish I wouldn't?

- What is something I don't do that you wish I would?

- What are my positive traits?

- What are my negative traits?

Reflect on any differences in your previous perception of yourself and how that might now have changed.

TRUST YOURSELF –
MAKE DECISIONS
BASED ON WHAT FEELS
RIGHT RATHER THAN
OTHERS' EXPECTATIONS

Dear... me

Writing a letter to yourself challenges you to think about who you are now and who you want to be. Not only can it enhance your self-awareness – and even encourage you to set some future goals – but it can also be emotionally freeing and help you to think critically about how you should live in the here and now.

Imagine what you want your life to look like in five years. Write it as an actual letter, and if you get stuck, try answering questions like:

- Who do I want to be, and how do I become that person?

- Where do I want to be, and how do I get there?

- What do I want to achieve, and how could I achieve it?

- Who do I want in my life, and how could I meet them?

When you are happy with your letter, put it away for a couple of days. Once you feel ready, look at it again and reflect on what your life looks like right now. Ask yourself:

- Am I on track to be where I want to be in five years? If not, what changes will make it a reality?

- What can I do today to make a start? How will my strengths and weaknesses help or hinder me from getting there?

Our lives are constantly evolving, so stay open-minded to a different future.

The aim of life is to live, and to live means to be aware, joyously, drunkenly, serenely, divinely aware.

HENRY MILLER

Chapter 2:

How to Master Self-Regulation

Self-regulation is our ability to control our behaviour and manage our emotions appropriately. It's a bit like having an inbuilt decision-making tool that helps us respond to situations in the correct way. It's why you show up for college or work every day, even though you don't always feel like it, or why you don't eat chocolate for breakfast!

Self-regulation is a key part of emotional intelligence because if you can manage your emotions effectively, you're more likely to benefit from a positive outcome, especially in challenging situations. So, if you're ready to regulate, read on!

Why is self-regulation important?

Self-regulation comes into its own when we're faced with a stressful situation or dealing with conflict. Managing your feelings and reactions gives your mind the space it needs to process the situation, listen to what your body and brain are telling you, and take other people's feelings and reactions into account. It also helps you cope with disappointment and react rationally when things happen that are out of your control. It doesn't get rid of negative emotions, but it does provide a framework for dealing with them.

How self-regulation helps us

Physically	Emotionally
Self-regulation helps us control the impulse to "lash out" in situations involving conflict and instead react in a more appropriate way. It also helps us stay calm during challenging moments.	Self-regulation helps us manage emotions. It can assist us in normalizing our feelings and then behaving more constructively. It also helps stop us from feeling overwhelmed by our emotions.
Mentally	**Socially**
Self-regulation is necessary in order to learn and perform a role. It helps us stay more focused on a task, listen to instructions, and switch our attention to different tasks when we're finished.	Self-regulation helps people behave in socially acceptable ways and build positive relationships by not letting strong emotions or impulses dictate their responses.

Reflect on situations in which you didn't self-regulate your emotions and the outcome was negative, such as a moment you "lost it" and couldn't control an impulsive reaction, or a time when you were disappointed. Create a table like the one on the opposite page and write an example for each heading. Consider what you could have done differently and write a short strategy to use to self-regulate in future. For example:

Physically

Example:

I got so angry with my sister when we disagreed over a financial problem that I shouted until I could barely breathe.

Solution:
When I realize I'm angry, I can stop, focus on my breathing, and then talk to her calmly.

Reflecting on our behaviour not only helps us see where we can get better at self-regulating, it also helps us become more self-aware. Self-regulation doesn't come easily to all of us, but if we can learn to slow down and take a moment to assess our feelings, we'll become more conscious of how best to modify our behaviour. This is the essence of self-regulation.

Turn pressure into something positive

An important skill for self-regulation is managing the effect that stress has on our lives. Remaining calm in the face of pressure isn't easy, but with self-regulation, we can make stress a more positive experience. For instance, some stress can focus and motivate us towards an end goal. But it can also be difficult to manage these emotions effectively, and if we become overwhelmed, it can result in negative outcomes, such as anxiety and depression.

Next time you face a problem and need some stress relief, try to **slow down**. It might seem counter-intuitive, but going more slowly gives your brain an opportunity to work through the problem. It's also important that you **acknowledge and accept the feeling of being overwhelmed**. Instead of fighting it and getting emotional, accept that stress can help you move past the negative feelings into problem-solving mode. Then, **get some breathing space**. Stop everything you're doing for a few minutes and focus on your breathing to collect your thoughts. Next, start **prioritizing and planning** your tasks. Having a plan allows you to focus on each step and keep a steady pace. Finally, **give yourself more time**. Reduce your commitments and designate more time for each task so you're not constantly lurching from one challenge to the next. Be kind to yourself!

In challenging situations, self-regulation can help calm the emotional part of the brain and engage the rational part so that you can work out solutions to manage stress.

Emotions are
like passing storms, and
you have to remind yourself
that it won't rain forever.

Amy Poehler

Resilience and self-regulation

Emotional resilience is not always about conquering challenges and winning battles. Rather, it's about having the ability to power through tricky situations and keep a level head. Resilience empowers us to perceive obstacles as "temporary" and bounce back from tricky circumstances without them affecting our internal motivation. It allows us to adapt our behaviour while also gaining the insight we need to avoid feeling the same way in future challenging situations. Learning to harness resilience is one of the most important skills for effective self-regulation.

Try incorporating some of these ideas into your daily life:

- Practise being more assertive and set boundaries (see page 150). If those around you are placing unrealistic demands on you, don't be afraid to say "no".

- Keep things in perspective. Try to look at day-to-day issues from a broader perspective rather than focusing on how a situation is impacting you.

- Be positive. Look for the good in difficult circumstances.

- Allow yourself to be imperfect – and acknowledge that each situation is temporary.

MANAGE YOUR
EMOTIONS;
DON'T LET
YOUR EMOTIONS
MANAGE YOU

Dialling down your emotions: part one

Disappointment that you got rejected for a job, a child in your care pushing boundaries while you're trying to juggle homeworking and life admin, being humiliated in front of friends or colleagues, or feeling the glare of disapproval from your partner or a loved one. We all have emotional triggers that can send us into a spiral of irrational thoughts and behaviours – whose only outcome is negativity and bad feelings all round. Emotional triggers often explain some of our most negative reactions, and can almost feel automatic, as though we've lost control of ourselves. But once you become aware of the types of situations that are likely to trigger your emotions, you can begin to develop strategies to help you self-regulate.

What triggers you? You might want to jot down your responses to these points on the opposite page.

- What frustrates you?

- What scares you?

- Do any situations make you feel resentful or disappointed?

- What embarrasses or humiliates you the most in life?

- Who or what makes you jealous?

- What situations cause you the most anger?

Often, we can't feel a trigger until it's been pulled. Start keeping a diary of your emotions – especially those provoked by specific situations – and you might begin to notice a pattern emerging in your behaviour. Jot down your thoughts to guide you ("He is SO annoying", "I feel terrible that happened", etc.), as well as your physical reactions (clenched fists, faster breathing, heart thumping).

Note any other factors, such as tiredness, hunger, alcohol consumption or illness, as these leave you vulnerable to being triggered more easily.

Start to become aware of the situations that trigger your strongest emotions, and then go to part two of this exercise, on page 56, for some tips on how to manage them.

Some people
want it to happen,
some wish it would
happen, others
make it happen.

Michael Jordan

History has shown
us that courage can
be contagious, and
hope can take on
a life of its own.

MICHELLE OBAMA

Dialling down your emotions: part two

Once you've identified your emotional triggers, you can start to think about how you can become better at self-regulating during those moments. While it's an easier option to avoid the trigger completely, this is often an impractical solution – unless you're planning on becoming a hermit – so it's really important to learn some coping strategies and be well equipped for whatever life throws at you.

Unless it's an emergency, most demanding situations need calm, rational thinking rather than an automatic emotional response – so you need to be able to stop, think clearly and respond in a purposeful, solution-focused way.

As soon as your body and mind start to respond emotionally – your body might tense up, and you might start to feel tearful or raise your voice with those around you – you need to start dialling the reaction down with self-regulation.

- **Focus on your breathing**. Hold your breath for five seconds to "reset" it. Then, take some slow, deep breaths, ensuring that the out-breath is longer than the in-breath to help slow you down. Repeat for a minute or two until you feel calmer.

- **Distract yourself**. Find something else to do for a little while. Take a short walk or go and have a shower. Listen to music or tidy up a room – anything that takes you out of the situation and allows your emotions to dissipate. Use the time to think of a more rational or positive response to the situation. If you have to deal with what is happening there and then, and you can't easily take a break, perhaps fake a need for a trip to the bathroom to give you five minutes to regain your composure and gather your thoughts before returning.

- **Let it all out**. Shout into a pillow if you need to! Or put on some musical belters and sing it out.

- **Think ahead**. Imagine you're waking up tomorrow after an emotion-driven reaction. Will you regret your response? Strong emotions make it difficult for us to see past the here and now, but we often feel differently once we've had space and time to consider solutions. Think of the impact your immediate reaction may have on your future self (and others), as well as the impact it's having right now.

Bad things happen to everyone. It's how we react that matters.

Anna Turney

Be aware of your thoughts and emotions,

and respond to them positively

A change for the good

The only constant we have in our life is change. It's probably one of the most profound paradoxes of our existence, as well as the most difficult one. Whether it's a change of job, a house move or starting college, change can unsettle even the most resilient among us and make us feel out of control. But if we learn to self-regulate those feelings, we can start to navigate change like a pro. Try these tips to help you see the positive in your next life change:

- **Acknowledge the change**. Don't fight it or deny it. Instead, step outside of it and tell yourself: "Things are changing and that's OK."

- **Even good change can be stressful**. Having a baby or accepting a brilliant job comes with stress, even though they are positive life events. These reactions are normal, so accept these anxious feelings.

- **Stick to your "normal"**. Keeping as close as possible to your usual schedule will help to "anchor" yourself when everything else seems upside down.

- **See the positives**. Change can present a great opportunity to "shake up" life with new influences. Whether it's new friends or colleagues, or an innovative approach to an old situation, change gives you the opportunity to grow and develop.

- **Ask for support**, even if it's just to vent or talk through negative feelings. It's OK to ask for help; it's a sign that you know yourself well enough to realize you need some assistance.

With the new
day comes new strength
and new thoughts.

Eleanor Roosevelt

Self-discipline dos and don'ts

Self-discipline is having the drive to deliver on our best intentions and goals, even when we'd rather be hiding under the covers or avoiding whatever we're *supposed* to be doing. In its simplest form, self-discipline is the ability to put off short-term pleasure (like going back to bed on a freezing day) in pursuit of long-term gain. Having strong self-discipline can help you reach personal and career goals and encourage you to take care of your physical and mental health, so it's vital to overall well-being, as well as being a big part of self-regulation. So, how do you get better at it?

Discipline dos

- **Do time-block** to get a task done. Put aside a set amount of time each day to work on your task or goal. Treat it as any appointment and show up on time, even when you don't feel like it.

- **Do remove temptation**. If there's something in your environment that's challenging your focus – get rid of it.

- **Do get an accountability partner**. Engage a loved one or friend to check in with regularly on your progress. They can help steer you away from temptation and towards your goal, as well as being a cheerleader.

- **Do know your "why"**. Explore why you want to be more self-disciplined and how it will benefit you, and use those thoughts to motivate you on your journey.

Discipline don'ts

- **Don't start big.** Don't try to achieve something huge as soon as you start your self-discipline journey because as soon as it seems hard, you'll lose motivation. Instead, work on daily or weekly goals, and once you've achieved them, acknowledge this with a positive gesture (like a fist pump) or a small reward, such as ten minutes scrolling on your phone or a biscuit from that jar.

- **Don't let a setback scupper your chances of success**. If you have a difficult day or couple of days when you don't achieve your intentions, don't beat yourself up and admit defeat. Instead, reaffirm that you *can* and *will* complete your task or goal. It was a side step, not a step back.

- In the same way, **don't let fear of failure discourage you**. We all experience failure and disappointment – they're parts of life! Learn from the experience and move on.

- **Don't forget to review your task or goal**. Goals can change over time and can also be affected by external factors beyond your control. Keep an open mind to how situations can shift, and take steps to ensure you stay on track by regularly reviewing your plans.

If you want to fly,
you have to give
up what weighs
you down.

Roy T. Bennett

EMBRACE NEW
OPPORTUNITIES FOR
SELF-DISCOVERY AND
DON'T LET THEM GO

Reframing negative thoughts

Negative self-talk (also known as "the voice of doom") has a lot to answer for. Not only does it pipe up at the most inconvenient and annoying of moments, but it can also follow us around, providing a constant negative narrative that would put a stuck record to shame. Self-talk is usually made up of a combination of past experiences and unhelpful assumptions we have about ourselves, others and the world we live in. Some common examples of negative thinking include:

- "I don't know why I bother; I'll never achieve that goal."

- "Everyone is bound to stare and laugh at me."

- "She probably thinks I'm weird."

- "If I have to speak in front of a room full of people, I'll go bright red and make a fool of myself."

- "I'm stupid, and I never get anything right."

- "My outfit looks awful. I should have worn something smarter."

It's important to know that thoughts like these are unhelpful and don't serve you in any way. Not only do they make you feel horrible, but they are also demotivating and stop you from living your life and enjoying it. If you can identify with any of the thoughts above, it's time to shut that negative narrative up!

Self-regulating our emotions also requires us to self-regulate our thoughts so we can sift out the unhelpful ones that encourage negative emotions. One of the best ways to silence the negative chatter and develop a more balanced way of thinking is to "reframe" your thoughts. It's a powerful technique used by therapists and psychologists, and it helps us to view any situation in a more calm or positive way. It's called the "Catch It, Check It, Challenge It, Change It" technique. It works like this:

CATCH IT: Catch the unhelpful thought. E.g. "I can't do this. I'm rubbish at this subject and should forget college."

CHECK IT: Check the thought: is it justified or exaggerated? E.g. "Last time I did a presentation, I was told that my nerves got the better of me, but I did get through it."

CHALLENGE IT: Challenge the thought: what evidence goes against the negative thought? Is there a positive thought to challenge it? E.g. "I was also told that the presentation was spot on, even though I was nervous, and I've been asked to give the presentation again."

CHANGE IT: Change it: is there a more balanced way of thinking about this? Can you reframe it? E.g. "I might find it hard, and I'll get nervous, but I coped last time, and if I plan really well, I'll be giving myself the best opportunity to succeed."

Now it's your turn. Fill in the table with an example or two of your own to help you reframe your negative thoughts and put things into perspective.

CATCH IT:
CHECK IT:
CHALLENGE IT:
CHANGE IT:

YOU ARE ENOUGH

Take a mindful moment

Mindfulness uses the gentle energy of our minds to alleviate stress. Finding a moment of calm in the middle of a challenging situation can seem like a difficult task. But practised consistently, mindfulness can provide us with the mental break we need to think and act purposefully when we're tackling big emotions and need to self-regulate. Next time your brain needs a break, try:

- **Observing**. Take a moment to really see what's around you. Whether you're sitting at your desk, on a walk or gazing out of the window. See the wonder in everyday things – the pattern on a teacup or the wind blowing through the grass. Such observations help to ground us and allow us a moment for a mental recalibration.

- **Listening**. In a world where communication is vital, how good are we at truly listening to other people? Be present while you're chatting with others. Really *hear* what they are saying, not just in terms of the words that they are speaking, but the feelings and intentions behind them.

- **Meditation**. Sit quietly in a comfortable spot and give yourself permission to pause and reset. To clear your head of unhelpful thoughts, focus on all your senses. What can you hear? What does the cushion feel like? What can you smell? Connecting to your body like this means you'll be less concerned with the thoughts in your head. Focus on the rhythm of your breathing and feel the calmness wash over you.

If you don't like
something, change it.
If you can't change it,
change your attitude.

Maya Angelou

Future perfect

Sometimes, our brains enjoy a trip to the future. Whether you're daydreaming about a planned holiday or fantasizing about what you're having for dinner, the mind's capacity to imagine future scenarios is one of the wonderful things about being human. It also means we can prepare for opportunities and threats in advance, therefore shaping the future to our own design, and giving us the best possible chance of self-regulating in tricky situations. But no one can truly know what is coming, so how can we use our daydreams to our advantage?

Cultivating foresight, and planning accordingly, can make the time ahead seem less uncertain and more likely to be filled with potential. Being able to consider multiple possibilities for ourselves can also help us make well-informed choices now. Futurism scholar Richard Slaughter defines foresight as "the ability to create and maintain a high-quality, coherent and functional forward view, and to use the insights arising in useful organizational ways". In other words, if we can visualize our future based on what we know of ourselves – our thoughts, emotions and behaviours – we can use that insight to formulate a plan to make our desires a reality. In essence, it can help us to navigate an uncertain and constantly changing world with purpose.

What does your future hold? Only you can make it a reality. So it's time to dream big and get planning! Remember, the actions we take now have consequences for the future. Make sure they're grounded in positivity.

When you release
yourself from
limiting beliefs,

you'll learn
to fly

Don't let disappointment drag you down

Disappointment is a feeling most of us can relate to. From *almost* winning the race to a date that didn't quite live up to expectations, or not getting that dream promotion – disappointment doesn't just leave us feeling flat and discouraged. It can also make us question whether it's worth the effort in the first place. These feelings are uncomfortable, but natural; learning some self-regulation skills can be useful when dealing with upsetting setbacks and get us back on track that bit quicker. After all, nearly all stories of triumph and success involve overcoming disappointment – the only difference is that those who do succeed in achieving their goals have learned not to let setbacks get them down and make them feel pessimistic about trying again.

Emotional intelligence allows us to see a positive purpose in disappointment. It is actually a really great tool for driving us towards our goal, rather than away from it. It prompts us to reflect on the situation and learn something from it so that we can move forward with adjusted expectations.

Dealing with disappointment

- **Acknowledge it**. Sit with your emotions. If it's making you feel sad and hurt, then allow yourself to feel that way. Cry if you need to. Accept that what has happened *has* already happened, and nothing can change that. But you *can* change your response to it.

- **Learn the lesson**. Think of the last time you were disappointed. What did you learn from that time? If you haven't already, take a moment to reflect on what happened, what went wrong and what you adjusted in your actions and behaviour as a result. You can use this insight to help you move on next time.

- **Tell yourself, "I'm going to move on now."** Dwelling on your setback keeps you stuck in the moment and unable to move past it, and it also encourages the unwelcome prospect of getting trapped in a negative thought spiral. Make a conscious decision to move on so you can start sussing out the positives and searching for solutions. Don't be tempted to berate yourself for what you should or shouldn't have done. Instead, reframe your thoughts to: "Next time I'll try..." Or, "It might help if..." Or, "I could..."

- **Anticipate future disappointment**. Consider formulating a Plan B next time, just in case things don't work out as expected. This is where foresight comes in handy (see page 72). Welcome other possibilities, and don't discount different options for yourself. You never know, it might actually work out better!

Open your eyes
and your heart to
a truly precious
gift – today.

STEVE MARABOLI

Don't let a permanent decision be based on a temporary emotion

Moving on when you're feeling mad

Motivational writer William Arthur Ward once wisely said: "Direct your anger towards problems – not people, to focus your energies on answers – not excuses." In the heat of the moment, when tempers are frayed and you've reached boiling point, it's difficult to direct anger appropriately. This is especially true if you're in a situation where you've been let down, wronged, lied to or badly treated – or, in fact, any situation that's prompted anger. Perhaps you're experiencing the break-up of a close relationship, or you've recently lost your job. You might even be dealing with the loss of a loved one. Irrespective of the original trigger, anger is one of the strongest and most difficult emotions to control.

But remember, anger is a natural reaction, and although it can be a little scary – not only for the angry person but also for everyone else involved – it can have a positive purpose, too. If it's expressed appropriately and is justified, it's a legitimate way to let other people know how passionate you are about something and how strongly you feel – ask any campaigner or protester. But while anger is a good motivator, it's also highly destructive if left unchecked. And even though you might feel so wound up that it's difficult to think straight – you do have a choice in how you manage your feelings.

Next time you're angry...

- Make yourself familiar with the physical signs. Perhaps you get short of breath, or your voice rises, or you get tearful. You might even shake a little. This is your body's way of telling you you're uncomfortable and you need to step away from whatever is upsetting you.

- Take some deep, grounding breaths. It'll help to bring your heart rate back down – and if you also mentally count your breaths, it'll distract your emotional brain and you'll switch to using your logical, reasoning brain instead.

No matter what happens in life, be good to people. Being good to people is a wonderful legacy to leave behind.

Taylor Swift

Chapter 3:

How to Be More Socially Aware

Improving our ability to understand others' emotions and reactions, and respond in a non-judgemental manner, can benefit us in all areas of our lives. Many of us know a "people person" – someone who intuitively senses how other people are feeling and what they're thinking, and can easily relate to them. Rather than "people skills", these individuals possess social intelligence, which is one of the key components of emotional intelligence.

In this chapter, you'll find guidance and tips that'll help you become more socially aware so that you, too, can forge close, authentic connections with those around you.

TO TRULY UNDERSTAND OTHERS, WALK IN THEIR SHOES, AND FOLLOW THE PATH THEY'VE ALREADY TRODDEN

The only thing worse than being blind is having sight but no vision.

Helen Keller

Why is social awareness important?

Many of us are familiar with the saying, "No man is an island." It's a 400-year-old sentiment that still resonates today – the idea that human connection is at the core of our existence and is absolutely vital for the well-being and survival of any individual. Studies consistently show that social intelligence leads to better relationship outcomes, effective leadership and professional performance in the workplace, and even enhanced physical health and general life satisfaction. Socially aware people share core traits that help them to communicate and engage with others in a variety of settings.

So, what do these super-social heroes all have in common?

Key signs of social intelligence

- **Conversational skills**. Socially aware individuals can speak to everyone with ease, irrespective of who they are. They're tactful, humorous and authentic, and never inappropriate. Their ability to remember details about people allows them to establish empathy and make the connection more meaningful. See the next page for some helpful conversation openers you can try if this is something you find challenging.

- **Active listening**. Socially intelligent people pay attention to what others are saying and really understand the meaning. They can also pick up non-verbal cues more easily and make others feel understood.

- **Ability to disagree without arguing**. People who are socially aware don't undermine others' opinions. Rather than arguing, they listen with an open mind and then express their own views respectfully.

- **Reputation management**. Socially intelligent people are aware of other people's perceptions of them. They can maintain their authenticity while also ensuring they create the right impression on others.

A good conversation opener can turn an average exchange awesome:

- Have you been to an event like this before?

- Tell me about you.

- How's the rest of your week looking?

- Are you planning a summer getaway?

- Have you worked on anything exciting/good lately?

- It's interesting/lively here. Have you been before?

- Have you tried [insert activity/restaurant/bar/etc., depending on the context of the event] before?

- Are you enjoying yourself?

If you're really stuck and it's starting to feel awkward, you can't go wrong with a statement about the weather!

Establishing empathy

Empathy is our ability to understand how and what someone else is feeling and thinking. It's a bit like when someone says, "Try walking in my shoes." What they mean is that they want you to recognize and understand the meaning and significance of their experience, along with what they are thinking and feeling about it. At the crux of this is *understanding* their unique, subjective circumstances while drawing on your own knowledge and experience of emotions and feelings so you can relate to their circumstances.

Here's how you can put it into practice next time you need to establish empathy:

- **Listen**. Validate their feelings by simply listening without interrupting. If they are telling you about a problem, don't try to offer solutions.

- **Communicate**. Even if their experience is outside your frame of reference, you can still empathize with managing difficult emotions.

- **Gentle gestures**. A sympathetic look or a gentle touch on the arm goes a long way. Simple body language often conveys empathy better than words.

When dealing with people,
remember you are not dealing
with creatures of logic,
but creatures of emotion.

Dale Carnegie

Open mind, open heart

Open-mindedness means being receptive to new and diverse ways of looking at things and being able to consider a wide variety of ideas, arguments and information. It helps us think critically and rationally about the world around us while also helping us to empathize with other people, thus making it a key component of social awareness. Open-minded individuals recognize that other people are free to express their beliefs and can acknowledge them without judgement. Most importantly, being open-minded helps us grow as individuals. We become more accepting of others, meaning we nurture more meaningful connections and develop stronger emotional intelligence.

You can expand your horizons by:

- Actively seeking out new experiences or information.
- Showing that you want to hear what other people have to say.
- Considering what other people are thinking.
- Being curious about what other people feel.
- Not getting angry when you're wrong.
- Being humble about your own knowledge and open to having it challenged.
- Believing that others have a right to share their beliefs and thoughts, and listening to them respectfully.

MISTAKES ARE
SIMPLY PROOF THAT
YOU'RE TRYING –
EMBRACE THEM

Social cues, social clues: part one

Developing our ability to identify and react to social cues is really important for building and maintaining relationships with other people, so it's a fundamental element of social intelligence. Sometimes these "cues" feel more like "clues" that we have to look for, particularly if they are non-verbal. For example, maybe you're having a conversation with a friend about a sensitive topic and their facial expression becomes a subtle frown – it's the clue that they are feeling uncomfortable about the subject, so you might want to adjust the conversation accordingly.

Social cues are important because missing them can lead to misunderstandings. If we're not tuned into other people's body language, it makes being emotionally intelligent that bit harder.

How to read the room

Pick up on subtle signals next time you're navigating a social situation by:

- **Paying attention to body language**. Notice posture and movements. What are they telling you about how that person feels?

- **Observing facial expressions**. The more we pay attention to other people's expressions, the more likely we are to see commonalities which help us notice the feelings of those around us more easily.

- **Tuning into tone of voice**. The pitch of someone's voice can help us to determine a person's emotional state and attitude towards us.

- **Gaining an insight into gestures**. Gestures are the physical manifestation of a person's intentions and emotions, and they are often used to emphasize or clarify what they are expressing verbally. A simple example would be a teacher telling their class to be quiet while also putting a finger to their lips. Try to pay attention to what someone is *really* saying through their gestures.

- **Maintaining eye contact**. Making good eye contact conveys interest and active listening, so if someone is looking everywhere else other than at you, and there is no obvious reason for it, then they may have lost interest in the conversation.

- **Watching your personal space**. How close people stand to one another can be a good indicator of how comfortable they are in each other's company.

- **The sound of silence**. Silence doesn't always have to be filled, or even feel awkward, as it can often indicate contemplation or agreement, depending on the context.

On page 94, you'll find some tips to help you become more adept at reading and responding to social cues so that you'll develop empathy and patience in your interactions with people.

The most important
thing in communication
is to hear what isn't
being said.

PETER F. DRUCKER

Follow your heart
but take your brain
with you.

Alfred Adler

Social cues, social clues: part two

With awareness, practice and a bit of patience, anyone can improve their skills at reading social cues. Whether you're a novice and need to learn the basics, or you're already a pro and need a quick refresher, try the following tips the next time you need to navigate a social situation.

Seven steps to social awareness

1 **Be aware of your surroundings.** Where you are determines how you're supposed to behave. For instance, if you're listening to your friend or partner give a speech at a wedding and know they're super nervous, it's probably a good idea to give them a thumbs-up for confidence rather than shout, "You can do it!" over the top of everyone's heads!

2 **Be a body language boss**. How do other people use their body language to communicate? Observe a verbal conversation out of earshot and see if you can work out what emotions the participants are expressing through their body language alone.

3 **Ask for clarification**. If you're in a social situation and can't interpret what someone is expressing, just ask them to clarify rather than make assumptions. It'll show empathy and active listening, too.

4 **Be empathetic**. There might be a good reason behind

someone's inability to read *your* social cues or follow social norms, such as an autism or ADHD diagnosis. They may not even realize their behaviour might be perceived as inappropriate or insensitive. Be kind and patient, and don't take it personally.

5 **Practice makes perfect**. The more you practise engaging with people, the better you'll get at understanding social cues. Seek out new opportunities to engage in conversations or attend social events.

6 **Be an active listener**. Active listening (i.e. *really* listening to what someone is saying) helps you understand the connection between what is being said and what is being expressed non-verbally. Don't forget to give your full attention to the person speaking and ask clarifying questions if you need to.

7 **Ask for feedback**. Identify areas for improvement by asking friends and loved ones for feedback. It'll give you an insight into how other people perceive you and, at the same time, a chance to practise your skills.

If you can master social cues, you'll be giving yourself the best opportunity to build meaningful and authentic connections with other people. This is the cornerstone of social intelligence.

True happiness comes from living as your

authentic self

Happiness is not
a noun or verb.
It's a conjunction.
Connective tissue.

Eric Weiner

Motivate and inspire

Being a cheerleader for the people around you builds connections and strengthens bonds. Whether it's a colleague who lacks confidence, or a loved one who wants to join a sports team but is worried they're not fit enough, motivating and encouraging others to fulfil their potential gives you the opportunity to support and bring out the best in them.

Motivating and inspiring other people is one of the fundamental traits of effective leadership, and it really comes into its own in the workplace, where recognizing potential and encouraging your colleagues to believe in themselves is crucial for team morale and productivity.

If it's your role to motivate others, often the best way to do this is to give people a reason to achieve. It sounds logical and could be as simple as engaging with their rational side by reminding them of all the benefits that await them if they succeed. But if you also want to *inspire* other people, you'll need to fire up their inner spirit and speak directly to their inner drive, which means connecting with their emotions and imagination.

Light their fire by:

- **Living your own values**. People are attracted to certainty, so if you show that you live your life true to your values, your passion and drive will inspire them, too.

- **Finding out what motivates others**. It could be different from what *you* think will motivate them. Consider what gets other people in your life fired up – what incentives help them get the best out of themselves? Listen carefully to their answers. Whatever makes them tick, remind them of it next time they need a boost.

- **Asking questions about someone** to uncover their innermost dreams and ambitions. Show an interest. Ask about their loved ones, hobbies or how they're going to spend the weekend. Their answers will show you what matters most to them and reveal personal traits you can leverage to inspire them.

- **Acknowledging challenges but emphasizing strengths**. Find out what worries the people in your life and encourage them to find solutions in their strengths so that they can overcome difficulties. Be upbeat and optimistic so that they know you believe in them and that they should believe in themselves, too.

- **Connecting on an emotional level** to provoke an emotional response. Talk to people about their passions. What drives them and makes them feel excited? Engage their imagination by encouraging them to visualize what is possible and then spend a moment picturing that future together. The aim is to provide a clear mental image for which they can aim.

- **Being supportive**. Follow up and provide ongoing emotional support to ensure others achieve their goals. Be their cheerleader when they're flagging and ask them how you can help. Let them know you're there for them, and you'll be giving them the best chance of success.

LIMITS EXIST IN
YOUR MIND – INSPIRE
AND EMPOWER
YOURSELF AND OTHERS
TO ACHIEVE

Only when we are brave
enough to explore the darkness
will we discover the infinite
power of our light.

Brené Brown

Be an active listener

We're all guilty of passive listening, such as when we accidentally switch off mid-conversation only to realize a few minutes later that we weren't really paying attention and we have no idea, let alone understand, what's just been said.

But *true* listening is an active process. You have to consciously put aside distractions and pay attention to understand what someone is trying to communicate. And it goes deeper because, to actively listen with emotional intelligence, you need to listen out for feelings, too, so you can build empathy and trust.

For instance, a friend is telling you about their partner's unreasonable behaviour. An active listener might say, "It sounds like you feel hurt and humiliated, and I sense that this isn't the first time." And the friend might respond by clarifying their feelings: "Humiliated? Actually, it's gone beyond that – I'm furious! But yes, I am hurt, you're right."

Get into the habit of listening as if you were going to repeat verbatim what the other person just said. It'll train your brain to focus. It's also helpful to restate part of what you've heard, such as, "Can I just clarify..." Also, watch carefully when they respond with non-verbal cues, such as tone of voice and body language, and notice whether these align with their words. If there's a disconnect, try asking an open-ended question, such as: "How do you feel about that?" or, "What else is on your mind?"

The best thing to hold onto
in life is each other.

AUDREY HEPBURN

Delivering disapproval with aplomb

No one likes being told they're doing something incorrectly, but just because criticism is hard to hear, it doesn't mean we should shy away from delivering it when it's justified. If someone has knowingly failed to do something, or has done it wrong or incorrectly, providing constructive feedback can result in a positive change in a person's behaviour or approach. In the workplace, where everyone has a role to play as part of a bigger team, providing the right sort of feedback to one person can have a positive impact on everyone.

Rather than only seeing what someone has done wrong, consider what they can do right next time. Offer solutions and positive suggestions rather than dwelling on their faults. Here are some tips:

- Don't just reel off a list of things they've messed up; think about what solutions you can suggest. For example, change, "That's wrong, and it's not what was asked for," to, "I can see you've given it a go, but I think there are a few areas we need to go back over. Why not try this?"

- Choose your words carefully. Avoid negative words, such as failed, terrible or bad. Instead, say, "It would be good if..." or, "This could help..."

- Don't deliver demands. Statements like, "You do this/that..." are unhelpful and patronizing. Speak in a calm, neutral way and simply say, "I would like you to do it this way..." or, "I suggest trying this..."

ACHIEVEMENTS ALONE
DON'T INSPIRE OTHERS
– IT'S THE JOURNEY
THAT MOTIVATES
THEM TO GREATNESS

Cultivating kindness

#BeKind isn't just a buzzy phrase used on social media; it's a whole movement that encompasses the idea that showing kindness and consideration towards others benefits everyone and creates a sense of community well-being. The thoughtfulness we practise through being compassionate to others is social awareness in action; it's a deliberate regard for the feelings and needs of other people.

And it's backed up by science, too. In an experiment led by American psychologist Elizabeth Dunn, a random sample of participants were given an envelope containing a small amount of cash to spend by 5 p.m. that day. Half of the sample were told to spend the money on themselves, whereas the other half were told to use the money to buy a present for someone else or donate the money to charity. When the researchers spoke to the participants in the evening, those who had spent the money on someone else rated their mood as significantly happier than those who treated themselves. Neuroscientific research also confirms that the warm, fuzzy glow we experience when we do something nice for someone else activates our brain's reward system. And we get the same positive feelings when we offer kindness to others as we do when we receive an act of kindness ourselves.

The key to being kind is to tune into your own behaviour, making sure it's having a positive impact on those around you. Look for opportunities to help someone out and be thoughtful in your actions and words.

Kindness in practice

- Try to anticipate what might make someone's day that bit brighter. If your colleague is drowning in paperwork, offer to get them a coffee. Or give a neighbour a lift to the shops if you know rain is forecast. Simple deeds pay dividends.

- Be considerate towards strangers, too. If you're on public transport, chat to friends at a lower-than-normal volume. Hold the door open for the harassed parent with the fractious toddler. Give them a smile and a kind word, too, if appropriate.

- Consider who in your life could benefit from some extra kindness – such as an elderly relative or a friend who's struggling – and show them you care.

- Be punctual and dependable. Showing up late or not making good on commitments or promises could be perceived as inconsiderate (and we're all guilty of it). If this sounds like you – and it may be unintentional – try to break the habit.

- Don't monopolize conversations! Give everyone a chance to join in. Ask what they think and how they're feeling, and really listen to their answers (see page 102).

EMPATHY IS THE STARTING POINT FOR TAKING ACTION AND EFFECTING CHANGE

Be thankful... not because life is good, but because you can see the **good in life**

Why gratitude is great

Think of the last time you expressed gratitude for something. Perhaps you told someone how grateful you were that they helped you out of a sticky situation. Or maybe you were just thankful for the support of a loved one and told them how glad you were that they're in your life. How did that moment make you and that person feel?

Gratitude can have a powerful and positive impact if we regularly incorporate it into our daily lives. Studies show that gratitude not only nurtures positive feelings, thus contributing to our overall well-being, but it can also have a profound impact on our emotional intelligence. One study published in the International Journal of Social Psychiatry in 2018 found that participants who felt more grateful and practised gratitude journalling were happier and emotionally stronger than others who did not.

It's really simple to incorporate more gratitude into your life – just try these tips:

- **Keep a gratitude journal**. Writing down the things you are grateful for is one of the easiest and most popular ways to welcome gratitude into your life. If you haven't got a notepad, you could download a journalling app to use on your phone or tablet. Try to make journalling part of your wind-down routine before you go to sleep so you can reflect on what makes you feel grateful each day. In time, you can revisit your journal as a way to remember those small moments of joy experienced every day.

- **Make a gratitude jar**. Write a daily note detailing three things you're grateful for and pop it in a jar. Over time, your jar will fill up with a myriad of reasons to be thankful, which you can use as a quick pick-me-up if you need a reminder of all the good things in your life. See the next page for some ideas to get you started.

- **Make a gratitude scrapbook**. Fill it with memories, mementoes and pictures that remind you of everything that's great about being you. You could even make one for a loved one and gift it to them as an expression of thanks.

I am grateful for...

New opportunities that come my way

The love and laughter in my life

The new day

Being able to feel the sun on my face

The support of my family

Fantastic friends

All the people in my life

The ability to learn new things

Having a place to call home

Having autonomy in my life

All the little moments of joy in my life

You cannot do a kindness
too soon, for you never know
how soon it will be too late.

Ralph Waldo Emerson

Gratitude helps us
to see the extraordinary
in the ordinary

Making compromises

Compromises pop up everywhere: finding a holiday that suits the whole family; the best way to complete a team project at work or college; what time you can politely exit the party when you're tired; and the mother of all compromises – agreeing with young children what time they have to go to bed without it resulting in tears and tantrums (from you, as well as them). It's safe to say the decisions we make in life are frequently reached on the basis of a compromise. Not only does negotiating a compromise offer the fairest and most diplomatic solution to a potential stalemate, but it's often a crucial factor in maintaining close relationships, particularly if continuing those relationships is more important than the outcome of the disagreement.

Compromise is best achieved if we're being emotionally intelligent. It's only natural that each person wants to obtain the best possible outcome for themselves, but recognizing the needs of others and modifying your demands accordingly – so that everyone gets something of what they want (but not *all* of what they want) – helps the decision sit comfortably with all while respecting each person's individual feelings and needs. It's all about fairness, considering all points of view, and mutual adjustments and understanding.

The rules of bending without breaking

- **Think the dilemma through.** Next time you find yourself facing a dilemma, reflect for a moment on what you want or need and on what you can compromise. What won't you compromise on? On what issue will you stand your ground?

- **Make your position clear**. State clearly what you do and don't want, and how you feel. Explain the benefits of your way of thinking and then listen, without interrupting, to what the other person does and doesn't want, as well as how they feel. It's really important that the other person knows that their feelings and views have been heard and understood so that a mutual decision can be reached.

- **Have a range of outcomes on the table**. If you can, offer several options that have varying degrees of compromise. For instance, if your partner wants to paint the kitchen fluorescent yellow but the thought of it is making your eyes hurt, a compromise would be to have one wall painted that colour while suggesting something a little more toned down for the rest of the room. Or compromise on having yellow appliances if the walls are a neutral colour. Or pick a totally different colour you both like!

- **Focus on the mutual decision rather than what you've lost**. The final decision might be acceptable, but not optimal. And this is OK, because the most important thing is that you've found a way forward. Satisfaction comes from achieving something rather than a situation leading to nothing.

Life shrinks or
expands in proportion
to one's courage.

ANAÏS NIN

Managing someone else's disappointment

Page 74 looked at dealing with disappointment. But what if you're the one delivering disappointing news? Whether sharing some bad news or having to let someone down, it's often as difficult managing someone else's disappointment as it is your own.

Fortunately, if you're emotionally intelligent, you can use your social awareness to manage the situation empathetically while managing any feelings that are hurt as a consequence.

Here are some tips on how to share some bad news with someone else in an empathetic and socially intelligent way.

Prepare in advance. Anticipate the other person's reaction and any questions they might have, and consider how you will manage this. Begin the conversation by saying, "I need to talk to you about something important..." then **explain the context** and what led to the situation, such as how the decision was reached or how the circumstances came about. Next, **state the bad news honestly** and acknowledge any emotions expressed as a result. Make sure your response reflects your understanding of how they feel (e.g. "I'm sorry this has made you upset. I can see how disappointed you are."). Finally, if you can, **state what you can do to help**, such as suggesting solutions and ideas of what they can do next to move on. Focusing on what can be done, rather than what can't, will give them the best chance of moving forward with a positive mindset.

DON'T BE AFRAID OF
FAILURE; BE AFRAID
OF NOT TRYING

Giving back

Getting involved in community or volunteer work helps cultivate empathy, as well as providing an opportunity for you to understand the needs of others.

Social awareness is a brilliant skill for the workplace, at home, at school or college, and when you're with your friends and loved ones, but it really comes into its own when used to help those in need. For example, working at a soup kitchen can help you understand the needs of the homeless; helping at a food bank will allow you to grasp the challenges faced by those living in poverty. Being altruistic isn't just part of our collective responsibility (as well as simply being the right thing to do): the insight it can provide into other people's lives is a gift that you can use to advocate for them and affect change in society – which is perhaps the ultimate expression of social awareness.

Life itself is a privilege.
But to live life to the fullest —
well, that is a choice.

Andy Andrews

Chapter 4:

How to Build Healthy Relationships

Positive relationships are vital to our mental well-being. Forming healthy connections with those around us leads to better outcomes, such as improved mental and physical health and an increase in our overall happiness – as well as a reduction in stress, anxiety and feelings of loneliness.

Relationships often take us to extremes of emotion, such as excitement, passion and love. But with the highs, we also have to accept there'll be some lows – despair, disappointment, frustration and all the bad feels we get when we're not managing our relationships effectively.

This chapter looks at how emotional intelligence can help nurture lasting connections, as well as identify and cope when relationships get tricky.

Relationships and emotional intelligence

You've already seen how self-awareness, self-regulation and social awareness increase emotional intelligence. But what's brilliant is that if we combine these three areas, we're able to enhance our relationship navigation skills. It's a little like stacking all the traits of EQ on top of each other, like building blocks, and now we're ready to put the final block on the top and link them all together – ta-da!

Effective relationship management involves making meaningful connections. It's not necessarily about making friends (although, by all means, *do* make friends if you enjoy someone's company) or finding a partner – it's about being able to work and exist collaboratively with other people, whether they're co-workers, an employer or employee, classmates, acquaintances, or the person you chat to every morning on the bus. It's also about understanding the value of getting along with the people around you – and perhaps also respectfully distancing yourself from those you've identified as having a negative impact on your well-being, whether at home, work or college. Here's a quick recap of why what you've learned so far is important for building healthy relationships:

Self-awareness

By becoming more aware of your own thoughts and emotions – through identifying your strengths and weaknesses, writing a thought diary and practising mindfulness – you've prepared yourself for healthier and more authentic participation in your relationships.

Self-regulation

By learning to control your impulses and regulate your emotions and behaviour – through identifying your triggers, dialling down your emotions and reframing negative thoughts – you're able to navigate disagreements and conflict, and present the best version of yourself in interactions with others.

Social awareness

Practising social awareness – by reading social cues, such as body language and tone of voice, and staying open-minded – allows you to become empathetic to the needs of others, meaning those around you are more likely to feel safe expressing their own thoughts and feelings. This, in turn, helps to establish mutual understanding and respect, so a healthy relationship is more likely to be the outcome.

So, what's the takeaway?

You've already done the hard work because relationship management is something that comes naturally once you understand the key skills of EQ. So, you can use these skills to recognize when something's not quite right in your relationships, or if you're trying to navigate a stressful situation or conflict in your team at work or among your college peers. The rest of this chapter will hone your relationship skills further so you can maintain close connections, even when the going gets tough.

Make conversations meaningful

Picture the scene: you bump into an acquaintance or colleague and they ask how you are. You say, "Fine, thanks. You?" and they reply with the same. Then there's a slightly awkward pause while you both wrack your brains for another comment to make, normally about the weather... Or worse, you launch into a monologue about all that's bad in the world. It's all a bit, well... pointless, albeit polite. Instead of making a connection with someone, the conversation crashes and burns, and you both end up feeling a bit flat.

Conversations are the medium through which we establish relationships in all areas of life. So, to make conversations really count, try the following:

- Be an active listener and ask questions. Welcome alternative ideas and opinions with an open mind.

- Try to avoid asking questions that will only lead to a straight "yes" or "no".

- Be authentic. Genuine interest will ensure the conversation moves forward.

- Use body language. Maintaining eye contact and nodding help to convey that you're curious.

- Don't look at your phone! The conversation is then doomed, as you're no longer listening properly, and you're also signalling to the other person that your phone is more interesting than they are.

Relationships take work,
and they take compromise
and compassion and
understanding.

CIARA RENÉE

Shutting someone up nicely

We've all been stuck in a conversation with someone who barely stops to breathe while they're talking. Whether they're bringing the conversation back to themselves or constantly moaning about the same topics, people who talk too much often miss the cues that their listeners are bored or frustrated. Any dialogue we were hoping for becomes a one-sided monologue, and irritation can then prompt us to give a rude response.

But you *can* get a handle on the conversation, and there are ways you can do it nicely. Here's how:

Listen closely. You need to be ready to interrupt when you sense a pause. Then quickly move the conversation on to a different topic or bring it to a close.

If this isn't possible, use body language to interrupt the flow. Touch their arm, if it's appropriate. Stand up if you were sitting down. Or, if you're in a meeting, hold up your hand to indicate you'd like to speak. Say calmly but firmly, "I'm just going to interrupt…" or, "I'd like to say something…" When you do get a moment to speak, **comment briefly on what they said so they know you heard them** and then take the conversation in the direction you want it to go. **Try to end on a positive note**. You'll feel better about concluding the conversation if you can say, "Thanks, that's really good advice – I'll remember that," or, "You've given me lots to think about."

SURROUND YOURSELF
WITH PEOPLE WHO
WANT TO LIFT
YOU HIGHER

Teamwork = dream work

Emotional intelligence is especially important in teamwork, where everyone brings something different to the party. Individual personalities and temperaments; eccentricities and quirks; different skill sets and experiences; strengths and weaknesses; and a variety of unique characteristics – meaning that the participants take on distinct roles and behaviours when in a group situation. It's called "group dynamics" and it can either make a team if the dynamics are positive (i.e. collective decisions are made, and everyone trusts and encourages each other) or break a team if the dynamics are poor (such as disruptive, self-serving or overly critical team members).

Dealing with different personal agendas is a common challenge in the workplace, at college and in social situations. Emotional intelligence can help you to read and understand what is happening and ensure positive outcomes, not only for the team as a whole but also for yourself. Here's how to give yourself the best chance of succeeding:

- Try to gain an understanding of other team members' emotions. Pay attention to verbal and non-verbal cues during conversations and observe how everyone interacts – it'll provide an insight into any stress, anxiety, frustration, boredom or enthusiasm people are feeling. What is this telling you? People who are in tune with each other often "mirror" the same postures and body language. Look for signs of mutual understanding and potential clashes of personality.

- See if you can help regulate other team members' emotions. For example, if someone is feeling anxious, validate their concerns and give them some gentle encouragement. Create an environment where everyone feels valued and listened to, by actively listening and showing empathy. A positive atmosphere will encourage open communication, creativity, ideas sharing, a sense of belonging and mutual respect.

- If conflict arises, or if personalities and personal agendas seem to be creating poor dynamics, ensure that everyone feels heard but then remind the group why you're all together, what you have in common and what you're aiming for.

- Make open communication the key factor. Check in with others, ask questions and share ideas. Solutions come from effective collaboration, and ensuring that everyone has contributed nurtures feelings of ownership.

A dream you dream alone is only a dream. A dream you dream together is reality.

John Lennon

Nothing can dim
the light that
shines from within.

Maya Angelou

Managing conflict

Conflict is a natural result of human connection. It's inevitable that when our unique personalities, values and life experiences are brought together, different viewpoints will occur. Emotional intelligence can help us to comprehend the emotions and ideas that fuel arguments and manage these situations with empathy and understanding. It can also assist us in finding solutions that move a challenging situation forward rather than accepting a deadlock.

Disagreements often arise from people's core emotions and beliefs but manifest themselves in a clash of opinions. So, it makes sense that if you use empathy to try to see the world through the other person's lens, you'll have a better chance of resolving your differences. This doesn't mean that you have to neglect your own values and beliefs, but rather that you should simply find some "common ground" and areas of agreement on which you can begin to find solutions that acknowledge the needs of both parties.

Keep the following points in mind the next time you find yourself at odds with someone, and you'll be giving yourself the best chance of resolving the dispute positively.

- Be assertive but not aggressive. Use statements such as "I feel..." or "I think..." This will enable you to convey your viewpoint while also respecting the viewpoints of the other person so that transparent discussions can take place. See the next page for some pointers on assertive communication.

- Look for win-win solutions. Emotional intelligence will help you seek out mutually satisfying outcomes based on shared objectives and points of agreement rather than one person triumphing over the other.

- Don't forget to self-regulate your emotions. Stay calm, take some deep breaths and pause to collect your thoughts before you speak. Keeping your own emotions in check is crucial for navigating a challenging situation.

- Use your emotional intelligence to consider the issue from all angles and keep an open mind to any solutions that present themselves.

- If you know you're in the wrong or you've overstepped the line, apologize sincerely. Emotional intelligence helps us to be accountable for our actions so that we can grow as individuals.

- If you're being apologized to, accept the apology and show forgiveness. Only then can the weight of the conflict be lifted, and you can both move on.

Being assertive

Being assertive doesn't mean being the dominant force in a room or coercing others into accepting your point of view. Instead, it's about voicing your thoughts and needs with confidence while still respecting the feelings and viewpoints of others. American psychologist and Holocaust survivor Dr Edith Eva Eger summed up assertiveness perfectly in her bestselling memoir, *The Choice: Embrace the Possible*: "To be passive is to let others decide for you. To be aggressive is to decide for others. To be assertive is to decide for yourself. And to trust that there is enough, that you are enough."

Next time you're in a situation that requires assertiveness, remember to:

- Use "I" statements to frame your views and root them in personal experience.

- Articulate clearly and calmly how you are feeling so that you invite the other person to understand your emotional state and mutual trust can be established.

- Communicate your boundaries respectfully while also respecting the boundaries and limitations of others.

- Encourage active listening and mutual sharing so that everyone feels safe expressing their thoughts, views and emotions.

Be assertive – if you don't take ownership of your destiny,

someone else will

Making new connections

In a world where familiarity feels safe, we tend to gather people around us with whom we're most comfortable. This means we naturally gravitate towards people who are a bit like us because it's the easier option. But by doing this, we're denying ourselves the opportunity to broaden our horizons, hear other points of view and share different life experiences – all of which enhance our emotional intelligence.

Meeting new people can be an enriching experience, and thanks to social media and digital technologies, it's easier than ever to stay in touch and keep those connections alive – so there's really no excuse!

You can widen your social circle if you:

- Get to know your neighbours properly – don't just exchange meaningless comments on the weather while you're taking out the bins! Invite them around for a coffee or plan a BBQ together, and if you get on, it'll be like hitting the neighbourhood jackpot.

- Join a new club or class – common interests are a great foundation for lasting friendships.

- Talk to strangers. Small talk can sometimes have big outcomes. Whether you're waiting for a lift or standing in a queue, just 30 seconds of chat can make us happier and healthier, according to psychologist Susan Pinker.

Successful long-term relationships are created through small words, small gestures, and small acts.

John Gottman

Maintaining strong relationships

To keep our connections strong, we have to put in time and effort. It sounds like hard work, but if a relationship is right for us, it happens without us even realizing. Nevertheless, we still need to make sure we nurture our closest connections – because when times are tough, it's the strongest relationships that really prove their worth. And it's often at our most difficult moments in life that we'll be thankful for the friendships and partnerships we've nurtured. This is how emotional intelligence can help:

- While interacting with friends, family and loved ones, be attentive – use active listening and read their verbal and non-verbal cues.

- Be sensitive to other people's emotions and respond accordingly. Provide support if it's needed and celebrate their achievements with genuine enthusiasm.

- Respect others' boundaries, values and beliefs – even if they are different to yours.

- Know that disagreements are OK, respect others' views and then work on a solution together.

- Communicate your own feelings and emotions. It's only by having an open dialogue with the people around you that mutual trust and understanding can be established.

How beautiful it is
to find someone who
asks for nothing but
your company.

BRIGITTE NICOLE

How to correspond with confidence

The ability to communicate with other people effectively is the thread that holds human connections together. But being able to know and understand the meaning behind the words being spoken or written calls for emotional intelligence.

Every exchange we have is an opportunity to strengthen connections, share ideas and experiences, and create the bonds that will enrich our lives. So, with so much riding on each and every conversation, how do we get it right?

Initially, it's important to recognize that different people require different approaches, and emotional intelligence helps us tune into these distinctions and modify our communication style to match. Some of us are verbal communicators who use words and tone of voice alone to convey our thoughts; others prefer to communicate their feelings through a combination of words, gestures and non-verbal signals, such as facial expressions. There is no right way, but being able to comprehend these variances and tailoring your response means you can have a conversation that really resonates.

It's also helpful to grasp whether someone is talkative and enjoys a lively discussion, or whether they're more comfortable reflecting on what others are saying before they join the exchange. This is particularly important in the workplace, where it's vital to establish a team dynamic that ensures everyone feels understood and heard. Allowing reflective talkers the space to listen, while also respecting those who flourish if they're given a platform for discussion, is emotional intelligence at work. Similarly, an introvert might thrive in small group interactions, whereas an extrovert will likely blossom in a large social situation. By catering for the needs of both groups, we can harness the power of conversation to build the strongest connections.

Here are some key points to help you communicate with greater confidence:

- **Be flexible** and try to initiate a conversation style that aligns with the other person. But be authentic – you don't need to change your accent or suddenly start gesticulating if it isn't your usual behaviour!

- **Ask open-ended questions** so the conversation is meaningful. When we ask closed questions, such as, "Do you have plans for dinner?" we risk the conversation coming to a premature and unfulfilling conclusion. But open-ended questions, such as, "What are your plans this evening?" invite the person you're speaking with to provide detail, and express their thoughts and opinions, without any restrictions.

- **Allow space and time for reflection**. Silence doesn't have to be awkward if it allows us to process what other people are saying, thereby understanding them better. EQ prompts us to pause so that everyone can collect their thoughts and respond authentically.

SURROUND YOURSELF
WITH PEOPLE WHO WILL
EXPAND YOUR MIND
AND HELP YOU GROW

Managing the "cold shoulder"

If someone you're close to has turned a little frosty of late and you can feel the chill, you're probably wondering why you're being subjected to the silent treatment. Whether it's a friend, partner, colleague or family member, being given the cold shoulder is frustrating because it denies you the opportunity to resolve a situation and move forward.

If you're confident they're not withdrawn because they're facing a personal challenge, you'll have already worked out that your silent friend is punishing you for a wrong you've done them. Ignoring you allows them to take control of the situation, and if they're feeling vulnerable, they may be cutting you off to protect themselves.

Here's how emotional intelligence can help to break the ice. Start by asking, "I feel like there's an issue between us, and you're upset with me." Then acknowledge their feelings ("I can see why you're hurt," etc.) and say how you're feeling ("I feel sad this happened," or "I feel terrible for what I did."). Be accountable if you're at fault and apologize, but tell them you want to work it out. Speak in a neutral tone that doesn't imply they're overreacting. Then, explain what you're going to do to put things right ("I know I let you down, and I'm sorry. Can I resolve it by...").

You can't fix the issue without their cooperation, so if they still won't engage with you, you might need to give them some additional time and thinking space.

No one becomes genuinely great by making everyone else feel small

TRUE FRIENDSHIPS MULTIPLY THE JOY IN LIFE AND DIVIDE THE ADVERSITY

Dealing with someone else's anger

Everyone gets angry – fact. Perhaps you work in a job that puts you in the firing line for other people's hostility; or maybe you've inadvertently upset your friend or your partner by saying the wrong thing or failing to do a task that you promised you'd see to.

Anger is a natural reaction when prior expectations or beliefs about a situation fail to materialize in reality – that's why we get so mad when we cancel plans and stay home, waiting for something to be delivered... and then it doesn't show up. The problem is that the part of the brain that's triggered when we feel intense emotions differs from the part that helps us make rational decisions. And the anger takes precedence – so if someone's been triggered, their ability to think calmly and reasonably has been temporarily switched off. So, if you then get angry at their anger, the situation can escalate really quickly. Here's how you can use emotional intelligence to avoid that scenario:

Use active listening and just let the other person get it all off their chest. Don't interject by saying things like, "Hey, that's not how I see it," or, "Hang on, that's unfair," and don't speak until they've finished, because interrupting them will annoy them even more. Once they've finished, **ask clarifying questions** so you can check you've understood why they're angry – for example: "Are you angry because we went overdrawn on the account or because I paid a bill late?" **Ask them what their expectations are now**, using a calm voice and non-threatening body language. State how you perceive the situation and how you're feeling. You might disagree or agree with them, and if their anger was prompted by something you know was your fault, now is the time to apologize for your actions – but you're not responsible for their angry behaviour or emotions. They choose to be angry, so the onus is on them to manage their feelings and reactions. **If you feel threatened or unsafe, leave**. Do not remain with them if they're so angry that they're scaring you or you're both too upset to attempt a resolution. Simply say, "I know you're angry, but you're making me feel unsafe, so I'm leaving now."

Whatever good things we
build end up building us.

Jim Rohn

Boundaries give you agency over your

body, feelings and emotions

Boundary basics

Boundaries help to protect our physical and emotional space, and they work best when we use our emotional intelligence to determine which ones are the most beneficial for us. This is important because if our boundaries are weak or too inflexible, we can start heading down an unhealthy path without even realizing it. But once we acknowledge our feelings and emotions by using self-awareness, we can set healthy boundaries that enable us to express our wants and needs while also respecting the wants and needs of others. Here are some examples that work for and against us:

Healthy boundaries	No boundaries
Being able to say "no" to avoid burnout.	Inability to say "no" to an unreasonable demand.
Respecting the needs and wants of others.	Not being able to accept "no" from others.
Communicating your own wants and needs clearly.	Not communicating your needs and wants clearly.
Respecting other people's beliefs and values when they differ from your own.	Being too rigid in your beliefs and values, and imposing them on others.
Being able to take time or space for yourself and your own needs.	Allowing someone to encroach on your personal time or space.
Being flexible without compromising yourself.	Putting yourself in an unsafe situation.

Everyone's boundaries are different. Often, they're based on a combination of beliefs, values, cultural customs, personal life experiences and family traditions.

To set boundaries that are rooted in emotional intelligence – ones that will therefore work best for you – you'll need to consider the following:

- **Goal setting**. Know why you are setting the boundary. For example, maybe you're taking on too much and need to start saying "no" before your well-being is compromised.

- **Practise setting your boundaries**. Especially if it involves others. For instance, if you need to communicate to your boss that you're working at capacity and can't take anything else on, you might want to rehearse what you want to say, as you might be feeling nervous about the conversation (see page 140 for some tips).

- **Keep it clear and simple**. Try not to overload someone with lots of unnecessary detail; focus on the main thing bothering you and deal with that first.

Setting boundaries can provide a positive balance and help you avoid burnout and resentment in relationships, especially if you love to help others out but struggle to do so without compromising your own physical and mental health. Boundaries also help you to keep yourself in check – especially if you have a deadline but can't seem to stay off social media!

Alone we can
do so little;
together we
can do so much.

Helen Keller

Spotting toxic traits

Toxic relationships can exist in many areas of our lives, from the college canteen to the boardroom to your own backyard. You can spot a toxic relationship based on how it makes you feel emotionally, physically and psychologically. If you feel anxious, unsupported, disrespected, humiliated or, at worst, scared, it's likely the relationship is in the toxic zone.

Sometimes, the signs are subtle. Maybe your partner speaks down to you and you feel demeaned, or you feel like you're constantly treading on eggshells around a judgemental colleague. The problem is that toxic relationships can cause long-lasting damage to your self-esteem and your overall physical and mental health.

Fortunately, you can use your emotional intelligence to mitigate the impact of a toxic relationship because your self-awareness helps you to acknowledge negative influences and look for solutions. Talk to the other person and be assertive about your needs (see page 134), and tell them how you feel using "I feel..." statements. Then, decide whether you want the relationship to continue and, if so, what behaviours need to change (possibly on both sides) to enable a positive move forward. Your boundaries can help you work this out (see page 150). Based on the outcome, you may decide you need to limit your interactions with the other person, possibly in the long term, if they are unwilling to change or you feel unsafe. Remember, the most important thing is prioritizing yourself and protecting your mental, emotional and physical well-being.

WE CAN ONLY
RISE OURSELVES BY
LIFTING OTHERS UP

A good friend is a connection
to life – a tie to the past,
a road to the future.

Lois Wyse

Life is precious:
be grateful for every
moment you spend with
the people you love

Farewell

Congratulations!

This may be the end of the book, but it's not the end of your emotional intelligence journey. Life is a fantastic opportunity for growth, personal improvement, self-realization and expanding our horizons – even when we hit a bump in the road. In fact, the bumps are the times in which we learn the most because the most fun is to be had in learning from our mistakes, celebrating our accomplishments (big and small) and transforming into the best versions of ourselves. Be inspired by what you've achieved, and know you can take inspiration from this book in the future, too – it'll always be here, waiting for you when you need it.

Every day is a chance to improve our emotional intelligence, and enhance our well-being and the happiness of those around us, so don't ever give up – because deep down inside, you know you've got this.

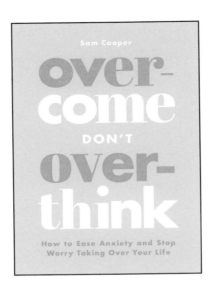

Overcome Don't Overthink
Sam Cooper

Paperback · ISBN: 978-1-83799-351-2

Say goodbye to overthinking for good

Everyone worries sometimes, but if you find yourself constantly overthinking every moment, decision and interaction, this can stop you from being confidently you. If you're someone who regularly feels trapped in a negative thought loop, this book can help you break this cycle of self-criticism so you can feel confident in everything you do.

My Daily Gratitude Journal

Paperback · ISBN: 978-1-80007-830-7

Invite positivity and appreciation into your life

Give yourself a gratitude break each day to remind yourself of everything you're grateful for, whether it's your family and friends, your health, your favourite TV show or even the weather. Once you get started, you'll be amazed by just how much there is to appreciate.

Have you enjoyed this book?
If so, why not write a review on your favourite website?

If you're interested in finding out more about
our books, find us on Facebook at **Summersdale
Publishers**, on Twitter/X at **@Summersdale**
and on Instagram and TikTok at **@summersdalebooks**
and get in touch. We'd love to hear from you!

Thanks very much for buying this Summersdale book.

www.summersdale.com